THEATER FUTURE DEVELOPMENT

JOHN LOK

Contents

Preface

Introduction

Nowadays, on movie and opera art performance lesiure market, our leisures businesses have many different kinds to let consumer individual choice, for example, movie, opera art management, football performance, swimming , bicycle competition performance etc. indoor leisure activities. How can persuade audiences to buy ticket to see any one of these indoor leisure performance? We need to learn audience psychological factor and indoor environment factor if leisure businessmen hope to increase their audience number easily.

Any theatre performance must need have good seats and hall facilities to let audiences to feel comfortable to see any performances, instead of facilities supply requirement. Audiences visual demand to actor individual performance, the actor performance must need to satisfy audiences visual leisure enjoyment. So, any global theatres must need have good performance hall and comfortable seats as well as every actor individual excellent performance skill to satisfy any one audience individual visual leisure need in theatre performance market demand and supply view.How theatre performances and facilities can attract audience individual leisure choice? In may this book , I shall attempt to explain how theatre management strategy implement in order to increase audience number. Readers can learn useful theatre management skills.

In my this book,I shall attempt to explain how to apply audience psychological and indoor environment factors to help indoor leisure activity businessmen how to entertain to achieve persuade many audiences to chooce to buy ticket to see their performance as well as how to design new space city tourism leisure to develop new traveller market. Readers can have more fresh lesiure psychological knowledge to know how to operate leisure service business.

Prologue

Table of content

Chapter 5
Movie and opera art performance leisure consumer psychology

ONE

PAST, PRESENT AND FUTURE THEATER PERFORMANCE DEVELOPMENT

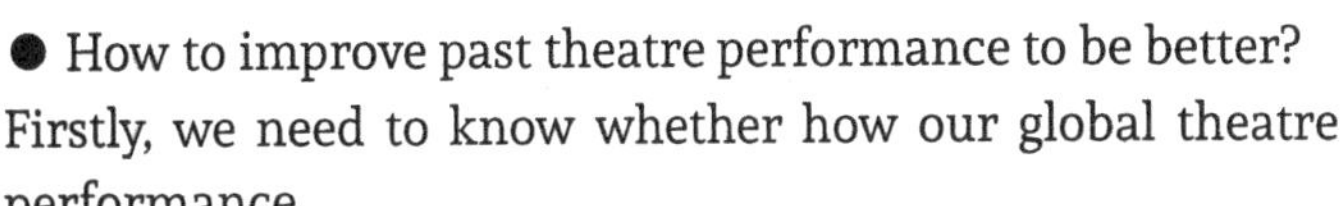

● How to improve past theatre performance to be better?
Firstly, we need to know whether how our global theatre performance
feature trends. In history of theatre charts , the development of theatre over the past, these performance developed into dramas, how did theatre change over time? As we explore how the theatre has changed over the years. We can see that in some ways the theatre has changed over the years. We can see that in some ways that it did not change that much. A thousand years after the first plays more staged, people still loved bawdy, explicit comedies

about society. Later in the restoration period, theatres began to stage so called " machine plays".

What is the history of theatre development ? History of theatre origins of Greek theatre, i.,e. in the levels of the followers of Dionysus, a god of fertility and wine. In the 6th century BC a PRIEST OF Dionysus , by the name of Thespis introduces a new element which can validly be seen as the birth of theatre.

How did Philippine theatre change over the years? After the Japanese occupation, the Philippine theatre has evolved to become an amalgamation of the3 various influences, such that of the Zarzela, comedia, Western classics etc. performances. By the 1950s, theatre had moved out of classrooms and the3 concept of paying for a ticket to see a theatrical performance emerged.

- What are the three origins of theatre development ?

The theatre of ancient Greece consisted of three types of drama:

Tragedy, comedy and Satyr play. The origins of theatre in ancient Greece , according to Arisotle (384 B322 BCE), theatre , are to be found in the festivals. Hence, our nowadays theatre performance is the evolution of modern theatrical production , we take a look at how the theatre has evolved over the year. In the past, theatre had been a welcome distraction. Trim tragedy, comedy, and satyr play performance mainly. In many locations, theatre as performance evolved from other ideas, such as old Roman philosopher , statue. Traditional theatre performance had been developed to today's digital performances in past forms of theatrical technology, due to theatre performance audience visual leisure needs (demand) had been changing.

- What makes a good theatre performance?

Today, theatre performance had been influenced by

audience visual leisure changing need. A great theatre performance is one where the characters are compelling . The characters will be the most recognized part of the theatre performance. They arte the people that act out the pitot and deal with the conflict and problems of the plot. The audience will mostly be interested in learning more about the character.

What is a performance in theatre? In performing, acts, a performance generally comprises , an event in which a performer, or group of performers, present one or more works of act to an audience. In instrumental music and drama , a performance is typically described as a " play" . A performance also describes the way in which an actor performs.

What is modern theatre feature? Modern theatre also known as 20th century theatre, impacting Asian, European and American theatre forms. It focused on a board perception of looking in to art, including theatre, critically, e.g. realism, musical theatre, opera are forms on new theatres.

Thus, theatre for development is a type of community-based or it is very important for actors and organizers of the performance or performance project. For example, theatre for positive youth development, theatre teacher needs to educate students how they see performance, which can bring positive social emotional to feel whether the theatre to let audiences to know. So, nowadays, theatre performance is needed to develop through drama. Theatre performance needs to provide visual leisure and education both aims, e.g. theatre actors and performance producers need to learn how to produce and inspire exciting and imaginative theatre, they aim to learn how to provide professional theatre performance production, education and training and visual leisure act performance development aspects, during the performance , the audience was asked what the actors reflected present community concerns and attitudes. A lot of work goes into creating a theatre performance. Today, theatres can generally be divided into two types: Producing theatres or leisure theatres. Producing theatres have creative teams which develop new productions from existing or new work, otherwise, leisure theatre aims to produce any kinds of visual leisure performance aim.

- Future theatre performance ought how to develop?

Future theatre performance tends on technology, scenographic performance, communal argument reality and the future of theatre and performance development and proposed how these might influence and benefit the development of theatre acts and lives, dramatic performance ,e.g. live performance theatres., they will continue to develop on appreciation for in-person experiences.

In the last few years, technological development likes virtual reality theatre and performance will be developed in their own visual leisure unique performance features to let audiences feel the different visual leisure enjoyment by technology performance improvement, e.g. smaller theatres can benefit from a wide range of societal theatres and develop it themselves . Also, in Western country, US , it tends to develop professional non-for-profit theatre field. In development a child's ability to understand the lives of others and fostering a deepe3r sense of compassion. Moreover, the future theatre artistic voice through the experience of live performance.

- How does technology transfer stage performance?

Other kind of future theatre performance development is

digital development in theatre. In theatre om audiences ,which will use their experience in theatre and performance on the digital music performance and video performance theatres both aspects. Future theatre industry will be experimenting digital performance. The future of theatre and stage performance is setting up digital kind of leisure performance, it may include: Venue planning, auditorium, seating design, digital performance production, specialist architectural lighting and performance sound, digital platform for the acts. If you are an individual audience customer, you will be influenced to choose to see digital theatre performance more than traditional tool to provide the act students with an in depth view of performances of essential. Rather than considering the real time or temporality of events, digital theatre concerns the interactions of people (audience and actors) sharing the same physical space (in an least one location, if multiple audiences exists).

The first digital theatre is founded in 2009, digital theatre is already the world's leading educational the world's leading educational platform for the performing acts. Today, digital theatres can provide 3 million students in over 2000 schools, colleges and universities across 65 counties with unlimited access to over 1,000 more full length productions and educational resources. However, digital theatre has provided free access to its archive of performances, it had been announced by their accounts managers.

IN the future, any one can watch digital theatre, we can watch digital performance on TV, desktop, tablet and mobile. Screen mirroring via a chromecast dongle from audience mobile or laptop. So, digital theatre can provide any audiences to watch performances in any places. It is a " live" performance placing at least some performers in the same shared physical space with an audience. Hence, digital theatre enriches and enhances the experience of watching a performance with exclusive . So, digital performances have the potential to open up access to the theatre to much wider population, when COVID 19 disease impacts theatres can nor permit open to let many people sit together in theatres. So, virtual performances can help theatres to keep functioning in lockdown or when outdoor performance. So , theatre and performance in digital culture examines the recent history of advanced technologies, including new performance leisure digital media. It will be accepted to watch an performance from desktop , laptop, mobile etc. technological performance platforms in the world.

TWO

WHAT PERFORMANCE SKILLS TO FUTURE THEATER PERFORMANCE INDIVIDUAL NEED

- What are theatrical skills?

The performing arts primarily focus on dance, drama, music and theatre. This means there's often overlap with the film. However, the skills that performer needs to be a performance artist. They may include: confidence, the ability to network and market the performer himself/ herself , self -discipline, on analytical mind the ability to self-reflect, flexibility , teamwork , organization and the management personal characteristics.

To develop a range of physical skills and techniques, e.g. movement, body language , posture, feature, coordination, timing, control, facial expression, eye contract, listening, expression of mood, awareness, interaction with other performers, dance and choral movement. Thus, performance skills are goal directed actions that a person enacts when performing a task. Focusing on performance skill is what makes occupational therapy's contribution to unique and powerful . Thus, making a good theatre performance , a great theatre performance is one where the characters one compelling. The characters will be the recognized part of the theatre performance. They are the people that act the plot and deal with the conflicts of and problems of the pilot. Also talent and technology is the most important skill to influence any one performer whose theatre music , dance, stage entertainment.

What are some life skills that are used I theatre? Life skills learned in theatre may include : Oral communication skills, creative problem solving abilities, motivation and commitment, willing to work cooperatively, the ability to work independently, time-budget skill. So, it implies that performer individual needs to learn right life skill and like attitude in order to achieve the excellent performances. Theatre performance ought have relationship to any one performer life experience. So., life experience is also one important factor to influence any one theatre performer's performance can bring more attractive or not to satisfy any audience's leisure need. Moreover, another kind acting skills are also important to influence theatre performance. Acting involves a board range of skills, including a well-developed imagination, of speech and the ability to interpret drama.

Another kind acting skills are also important factor to

influence any one theatre performer's performance can bring more attration or not to satisfy any audience 's leisure need. Moreover, acting involves a board range of skills, including a well developed imagination, emotional facility , physical expressivity, vocal projection , kind clarity of speech and the ability to inteerpret drama, another kind is performance skills, performance skills are goal-directed actions that a person enacts when performing a task. It causes on performance skill is what makes occupational therapy's contribution to unique and powerful.

- main elements influences theatre performance

Thus, to achieve the best theatre performance objective, the three basic elements of theatre may include : performers, audience , director, theatre space, design aspects (scenery, costume, lighting and sound), text which includes focus purpose point of view. However, the most important life skill , any one performer needs to learn in theatre is communication. Many theatre performers develop the ability to speak clearly, incidly and thoughtfully . When the performer acts on stage , he is comfortable speaking to range groups of people. Many theatre companies look for this in an individual when individuals who can demonstrate excellent verbal and written communication skills, teamwork, and attraction performing actions in order to satisfy audience leisure need, when they decide to buy ticket to see the theatre performance show.

Thus, when a theatre student hopes to learn theatre skills easily or understands easily. He/she ought have these psychologicall attitufes: Self awarenesses, being open and receptive to criticism, teamwork, time management, dealing with all types of different people, confidence and public speaking skills, being realistic. He also needs to know whether he ought how to learn theatre acting, such as learn to use masterclass, read actor biographies or autobiographics, be more abservant of people in action, listen to podcasts, teach others, study people who are like what skills the perfrmer can learn from drama. Drama promotes communicataion skills, teamwork,dialogue, negotiation, socialization. It stimulates th imagination and creativity. It also develops a better understanding of human behavior and empathy with situations that might seem distant. Performance skills in drama may include: movement-soft, gentle, heavy light , quick show, resture signals with your hands/arms to show feelings, facial expressions wide eyed, norrow eyed, raised eyebrows, troubled permanent frown, down turned mouth, eye contact staring, glaring fleeting, voice-pitch high and squeaky , low and soft etc. body language skills.

In fact, students involved in drama performanc coursework when one student decides to learn theatre performance or experience outscored non-act students. Drama can improve skills and academic performance in children and youth with learning disabilities . Because the practical role performing acts plays in a well-rounded. It's about learning transferable life skills. By observing others students learn to make creative choices on stage by creativity and imagination. So, Drama classes can give performance chance to let theatre students to attempt to improve their performing skills. Also, drama enhances students' artistic and creative abilities and gives them a better performance improvement through learning which involves thought, feeling and action, workshops and attendance at theatre performances.

On conclusion, the performing acts primarily focus on dance, drama, music and theatre perforforming acts students can develop skills needed for life and music, theatre, and speech and debate activities are ideas for them to learn through intensive research not just facts and every time performance learning courts can let they have performance practice experience to improve their next performance more attractive. Hence, every time theatre performance practice can help any theatre students to improve thwir life skills, acting skills , performance skills absolutely.

THREE

THEATER PERFORMANCE BRINGS WHAT SOCIAL BENEFIT

● Why do our society need theatre performance?
What benefits of music, drama, dance, act performance , they can bring benefits to our society? How they can impact our social future development? What negative impacts, they will influence to our social development? I shall attempt to answer these questions concern future theatre performance whether it ought continue to develop or not.
Theatre can improve social bonding, allow do emotions to be explored in a safe space, develop the emotional and cognitive skills to deal with a complicated world, and kick-start coversations about important issues. How does theatre contribute to society? The theatre , dance and other performing arts can teach people how to express

themselves effectively and can also be a tool though with people with disabilities can communicate. In addition to teaching self-expression, the performing arts, help society or a whole in self-knowledge and understanding.

What is the purpose of theatre for social change? It is unlike other kind of theatre, theatre for social change is a performance to raise awareness about the impact of social issues through community engagement process. How does theatre have an economic impact on society? Theatre and performing arts are also hugely imported to economies and brings societies positive impact. The US Bureau of economic analysis showed that 3.2 % of US GDP around US$504 billions is attributable to arts and culture (compared with the entire US travel and tourism industry, which accounts for 2.8% of GDP).

Hence, in theatre performance, originally a supplemental performance by an actor or actress, who kept all or past of the theatre performance. The benefits of drama performance, the benefits are physical , emotional , social and they help to develop , health society in many cases the quality of any performance reliance on an performance.

- Threatre performance brings what beneftis to impact our future social development ?

some benefits include emotional, social , physical and even academic aspects, instead of economyic benefit to societies. What are theatre performance emotional benefit? On student theatre performance educstional aspect, a range of emotions and encourage them to understand and deal with similar feelings . They may be experiencing, aggession and tension are releases in a sage , controlled theatre performance learning environment. So, there are five benefits to students who participate in theatre arts. They may include: helping them to build empathy emotion, whe kids participate any characters playing in thetre performance. They can learn how to control emotions to keep calm more than engry feeling or emotions in any future working environment easily when they need to work in society.

Improvement academic performance, participation in drama boosts students feelings of belonging and keeps them motivated at school, building goal-setting direction mind, self-esteem. All of these positive emotions, any student may be influenced when he/she can spend time to participate any kinds of theatre performance learning chance. So, the main purpose of theatre performances i s that , in fact, the purpose of theatre is to provide through job to people. The threatre is a branch of the performing arts and it is concerned with the acting our stories in front of the audience. The benefits of performing arts include improving life skills and academic performance to students.

- How can watching theatre benefit the mind?

These who watch live theatre have a reduction of stress and tension. The experience is to immersive that the audience can quickly become in the show. Live theatre allows you to forget about your daily stresses and feel as peace when you are watching in theatre hall. Hence, the benefits of drama for children, a good understand of characters, roles and subtext of plays will allow childrens' emotional intelligence building through the use of imagination, also live performance could also provide a host of developmental benefits, including improved emotionable child,individual can also bring emotional intelligence from theatre art performance learning, it focuses students can spend how much time to participate in youth theatre and still loves to attend live performances.

What re theatre performance social benefits? community theatres involves more participants, present more performances of more. Participation in community theatre brings with it on immediate social circle, and all the networking benefits. How does theatre contribute to society? The theatre, dance and music and drama etc.performance acts can teach people to express themselves effectively, and can also be a tool through which people with disabilities can communicate . In addition to teaching self-expression, the performing arts help society as a whole in self-knowledge and understanding can theatre bring positive and/or negative social change?

Theatre for social change is one of many frameworks that can be used to solve problems and create changes in society. However, the unique part of the theatre , which utilize and engage directly with the full human body. Horeover, theatre performance can let many studetns feel that theatre helps them develop the confidence that's essential to speaking clearly, lucidly and throughfully. Acting onstage teaches students how to be comfortable speaking in front of large audiences, and some of student theate performing learn classes will give them additional experience telling to groups.

- What physical benefits can bring to individual from theatre performance?

Instead of theatre performance can bring social, economic emotion benefits to society , student individual emotion, economic income growth. Whether theatre performance can bring benefits to audiences when they buy ticket to watch any kinds of theatre performance in theatres. How can watching theatre benefit the audience individual mind?

Theatre encourages and expresses emotions in their most extreme form. As a human, watching any kinds of theatre performance or listening any kinds of music performance in theatre, others express emotions can trigger that their emotion repsonse in audience individual feeing as well. Theatre shows healthy to let any one audience to feel all types of emotin and to understand empathy. So, it seems that theatre is not only entertaining, but also has both mental and physical health benefits crucial for a healthy lifestyle. When audiences who attend performing arts events are healthier, have lower anxiety, and are less likely to suffer from depression.

- Can theatre performance improve studend individual academic performance?

Can student often watch theatre performance to improve his/her academic performance? It seems that these questions concern whether watching theatre performance, which can boost academic performance. It shows that educational psychologists believe that engaging with performing arts can boost the academic performance of the average child by 4 % when drama is part of curriculum.

The social benefits of theatre and performance include better self-efficiency in children and teenagers, as well as making them better equipped to broach complex subjects. How does theatre help education? Using drama and theatre as a tool to teach is not only effective, it will also bring the necessary change in the learning process for students. This concept helps students learn better, instead of simply being observers. They get to be a part of the learning process. So, theatre can enrich, student individual life, because these it does not harm, expresses a basic human instinct, brings people together models democratic discourse, contributes to education and literary , sparks economic revitalization, and influences how we think and feel generation's learning life.

- How do the arts improve academic performance?

Student s that like a combination of arts programs demonstrate improved verbal, reading, and math skills, and also show a greater capacity for higher ordered thinking skills, such as analyzing and problem solving. How can theatre help student learning development in his/her learning living experience? Many students find that theatre helps them develop the confidence that is essential to speaking clearly and thoughfully. Acting on stage teaches student how to be comfortable speaking in front of large audiences, and some of students their theatre classes will give them additional experience talking to groups. The recent university university research explored the educational and social benefits from theatres, theatres can improve social bonding, allow for emotions to be explored in a hallpy life environment. So, students can improve their communication skills and their capacity to read -write and speak when they can attempt to spend some extra time to participate to learn theatre performance in schools.

I means that little time spending theatre performance learning participation , it can improve student individual academic performance in possible , other excess time spending theatre performance learning participation it can not improve student individual academic learning performance, even it can bring worse academic result, because busy theatre students, involved in a production or other theatre projects when also taking a heavy academic load. So, I believe that theatre performance learning participation ought improve any student individual academic performance, but it depends on whether he/she spends some extra little time to particpate any kinds of theatre learning performance or spends more time t participate any kinds of theatre learning performance. It is value research whether theatre performance how to influence academic performance on education issue aspect.

FOUR

AUDIENCE CHOICES BETWEEN THEATER AND CINEMA MOVIE LEISURE

- Supply and demand view to future theatre and cinema movie leisure industry

In audience behavioral leisure psychology view, when the audience consumer has time to spend watching lesiure activity. When he feels leisure time is less , he will make watching lesiure either he makes purcahse ticket decision to enter cinema to watch movie or he makes purchase ticket decision to enter theatre to watch art performance, So, it seems that any kinds of movie may be any kinds of art performance competitors. Howwver, those factors may influence theatre performance audience number, they may include whether that art performance is attractive to satisfy audience's visual leisure feelingl, how many movies number is supplied to cinemas or how many art performance number is supplied to theatres, how many audiences number choice to buy ticket to watch art performance or, watch movie.

So, it implies that movie number may influence theatre art performance audiences number because watching leisure audiences may watch any kinds of movies or theatre performances. In supply and demand view , it explains when the consumer feels watching leisure need in any holiday, he needs either to watch the movie or watch the theatre performance. Hence, whether the month has how many movies have already been watched by audiences in cinemas. Their movies number may absolute influence theatre performance audiences choice to watch which movie in order to replace any one theatre performance.

Hence, any one theatre performance provider, whose competitors may include other theatre performance providers and other movie providers both , even online theatre performaners, because any one audience may choose to watch art performance from internet channel. Hence, future theatre performance market competition is serious. I believe that instead of whether the theatre performance arrangement is attractive factor, ticket price is resonable factor, performance time factor, the theatre design facility factor may also influence audiences wathing to the theatre performance choice.

It means that theatre facility environment may be one

influential factor to persuade audiences to enter the theatre to watch the art performances. If the theatre facility environment light and sound facilities are not supplied enough to satisfy audience 's listening and watching feeling. They can not sit comfortable in the theatre seats. Any of these external theatre environment facility factor also may influence audiences number to the threatre. So, future theatre environment facilities must be needed to raise quality in order to achieve the high service enjoyable level to satisfy audiences leisure need, e.g. electronic moving seats, they can let audiences have auto rising or fallig feeling when they are still sitting on the seat in theatres. Music must need soft music, it can not permit loud in theatre environment, because soft music can let audiences to feel comfortable to watch and listen any kind of art performance. The art performance time can not perform too short time, e.g. half hour, but performance time can not be long time, e.g. more than two hours, because the art performance time is too short , it will let audiences feel ticket price is too high, but if the art performance time is too long, it will let audiences feel boring when they need spend long time to sit on seats.

Hence, any one art performance time is also one important factor to influence audience individual leisure feeling. Moreover, any kinds of theatre art performance must need have educational aim. It means that the art performers must need to let students feel that they can learn knowledge to be applied to their life experiences after they watched the art performance, because nowadays, many audiences are young, they choose to watch the kind of art performance, they need have leisure feeling and learning new life experience knowledge from the kind of art performance, because some young people choose to watch the kind of art performance, they hope to learn new life experience knowledge in order to pursue art performance career.

So, whether the art performance can let th young student to feel that he can learn art performance skills or not, it will influence the art performance learner to choose to watch the kind of art performance or not. Hence, whether the kind of art performance, it has educational feelingto the art performance learning audience, it will influence whether the art performance learner to choose to go to theatre to watch the art performers; performance in theatre, because if the art performance learners feel the kind of art performance can not let them to feel they can learn any new art performance skill, they won't choose to buy ticket to watch the kind of art performance. So, any one art performance provider must need to consider performance leisure and performance educational both aims in order to satisfy art performance lesiure audiences and art performance learner audiences their psychological needs.

In fact, instead of lesiure art performance audiences, learning art performance, they will be another main audiences source, such as art performance students, because they need to go to classroom to listen art performance teachers to learn any kinds of art performance skill, they also choose to buy ticket to watch any kinds of art performance because watching art performance may be another kind of learning art performance skillful method to raise improve their art performance skills, So , future art performers need to know how to perform in order to satisfy art performance student individual learning need. So,, future any art performance students may be any one art performance service provider 's audiences. They can not neglect this new art performance student audience group in future art performance market development trend.

On conclusion, when art performance students feel the kind of art performance can satisfy their art performance skill learning need. They won't choose spend much time to buy ticket to enter cinemas to watch movies, even if the kind of art performance service leisure provider can provide any kinds of attractive art performance to let audiences to watch, as well as the theatre facilities can be improved more comfortable feeling, then many movie audiences will be persuaded to buy ticket to enter theatres to watch any kinds of art performances.

So, future theatre performance market development success depends on art performer individual performance skill, theatre facilities service improvement, art performance ticket price and performance time factors. Also, the difference between movie performancers and art performancers is that movie performaners can not do "life show". Otherwise, art performancers can do life show, life show is one kind of life experience, every art performer needs to do life experience, perform on theatre, they can have immediate emotion feeling from audiences whether they like their art performance or they dislike their art performance. When they are performing life show in theatre.So, their satisfactory feeling ought be more than movie performers. Moreover, art performance behearsal time ought be more than movie performance rehearsal time, if they hope to perform the most effective result. Hence, art performance market, it still have these strengths to win movie audience individal leisure choice in global art performance theatre market.

FIVE

MOVIE AND OPERA ART PERFORMANCE LEISURE CONSUMER PSYCHOLOGY

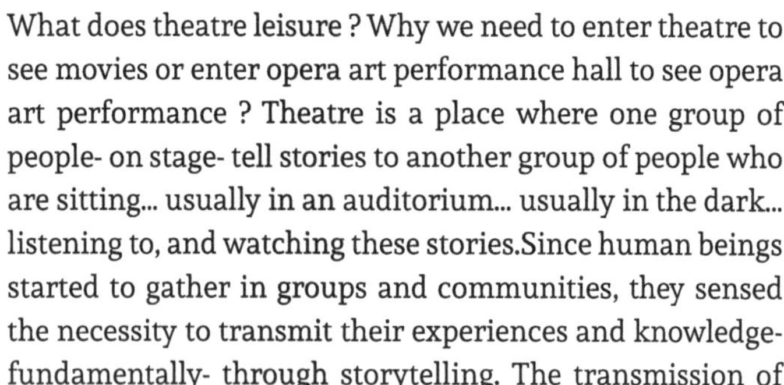

What does theatre leisure ? Why we need to enter theatre to see movies or enter opera art performance hall to see opera art performance ? Theatre is a place where one group of people- on stage- tell stories to another group of people who are sitting... usually in an auditorium... usually in the dark... listening to, and watching these stories.Since human beings started to gather in groups and communities, they sensed the necessity to transmit their experiences and knowledge- fundamentally- through storytelling. The transmission of these stories, through the ages moved from shamanism to modern forms of art on and off stage.

Theatre is a tool that has existed for thousands of years. I imagine that from the first moments people wanted to transmit their experiences of the hunt, or their father and grandfather. It is both the wish and necessity of human beings to tell stories.Theatre is an art form that brings people together to celebrate, challenge and provoke through the telling of stories. Theatre is unique, you see transformation right in front of you- created in the moment. In a book; you pick it up, put it down and it remains – similarly with film- but with theatre, what you witness in any given moment is unique and only you and the audience will ever experience that.Theatre is a moment of intersection between people where events collide or reveal conflict through storytelling. It is an art-form that always has, and always will be, important and relevant.Theatre is a sense of escape, it transforms you into a new space. It can however, be many things. Theatre can be a source of intellectual learning, inspiration, and can even reflect your life.Theatre is live, and that's important. So much of our art is consumed through live-streams, through computers and so on – and this misses that extraordinary atmosphere, and sense of grounding and presence that theatre gives.

Why do we need to see opera art performance? Going in front of an audience- be it small or large- is a performance?you have to captivate people with what you say, do or whatever! This is the basic of performance.Not everyone can perform. The people who do it have a virtue that they can exploit to get that attention from people. Performance is about having the capability to captivate an audience with whatever means you can see with words, theatre, dance, music and so on.

What does leisure consumer behavior? How to persuade leisure consumer individual feels to enjoy the kind of leisure activities? I shall attempt to indicate art opera performance or movie lesiure example to explain how to persuade audiences feel leisure enjoyment to see the movie or see the opera art performance. For movie or art performance leisure, instead the movie or opera art performance, the artors individual performance attitude whether they can attract any audiences that they can feel enjoyment or leisure seeing feeling and the movie or art opera performance content whether they can attract their leisure emotion factor, the movie and opera art performance whole length of time factor is also important because if the movie or opera art performance time is too long, e.g. above two hours, then the long time movie or opera art performance can not persuade audiences to feel attractive, otherwise, they will feel boring when they feel that they need to sit more than two hours time to see the movie or see the art opera performance in the cinema or art opera performance hall. Unless, the audiences feel very enjoyment to see the movie or art opera performance.So, it explains why general movie or opera art performance time can not exceed two hours. Because instead of performance cost reason, audience individual boring feeling reason is another important audience leisure psychological factor to influence whether the movie or opera art performance can attract or persuade many audiences to choose to to buy ticket to see the movie or the art opera performance.

CINEMA MOVIE AUDIENCE LEISURE PSYCHOLOGY

Theatre is a collaborative art-form with writers, producers, directors, lighting designers, costume makers and so on. When all those pieces coincide, and when the performances are great, the lighting is great, the music is great, the design is great.... when all those different creative activities fuse into one emotional and intellectual delivery- that's when great theatre occurs.

Different films need to arrange different audience individual leisure taste to adapt their seeing movies or opera art performances raising enjoyment feeling.Each year a small number of new release films, 6-10 titles, become 'events'. These films such as the new James Bond, the latest Disney family feature and other big action titles such as the Marvel films or 'sagas' such as Twilight and The Hunger Games, are the bedrock of commercial cinema. These are mass appeal films created at huge cost and supported by massive marketing effort. They provide a disproportionately large amount of a cinema's annual income and they generally appeal strongly to the youth audience (16-24 year olds). 'Event' films are shown widely at multiplex cinemas but often perform poorly in local independent cinemas when shown a few weeks after the initial high profile release although some people will be prepared to wait if they have seen the film trailered at a favourite cinema.

In contrast a large number of high quality, independent and foreign language films are released annually but invariably they earn much less at the box office. These films appeal more to 30+ year olds and can prove to be very popular with particular audiences in individual cinemas. However,in recent years the 45+ age group has become one of the largest growth markets in UK cinemas with films such as The Best Exotic Marigold Hotel with more mature characters and strong storylines aimed at a multi-generational market. Young people, although still the multiplexes mainstay audience, are increasingly consuming film online through downloading or streaming services.

In fact, films based on literary works or specific aspects of social history or parts of the country are often well received by local audiences who prefer cinemas with comfort, character and the opportunity to have a coffee or a bar drink.Young children enjoy cinema going. Sometimes they attend with a group of friends. Often they are accompanied by parents or relatives. Films for the younger age groups are important for local cinemas and may attract sell-out audiences for morning or matinée performances, especially at weekends and during school holidays. Many cinemas now have a regular slot for this audience and operate it like a 'club' to encourage repeated visits. Local cinemas have to be capable of adapting to whatever is currently in the news and available to them. This requires skill and showmanship on the part of the cinema manager and staff in addition to a well designed building.

Why has theatre become such an important art-form?

In my imagination this goes back to the time when we lived in caves. I'm pretty convinced that two people, three people or one person sat on one side of a fire, providing the lighting- while a lot of other people sat on the other side of the cave or dwelling... and from time immemorial stories were told by one or several people, to a larger group of people. These stories may have been history, myths or legend.... they may even have been about religion or about grappling with the seasons.

Stories have always been told by live human beings to other live human beings, that's what makes it such an important and enduring form of art in my view.The unique selling proposition of theatre is the fact that there are live humans in a space, speaking to other live humans. It's not online, not in a cinema, not on some tablet... it's there. As a member of the audience, you are in the same space as the people who are- in the broadest sense of the word- telling stories. The very fact that humanity is at the absolute centre of theatre in tangible flesh and blood terms means that there is intrinsic beauty in that art-form because the human form, human voice and human ability to imagine stories (and their repercussions) is the stuff of art!

The aesthetic and beauty of theatre are very subjective. Performance and theatre can take many forms. It may be a play on the street or- as you saw during the early 19th century- a form of Opera where many forms of art were gathered into a single performance. The aesthetic of the elements of a performance when they are brought together depend on the culture of the people receiving it and where the piece itself is performed.The aesthetic and beauty of a piece of theatre lies almost completely in the eyes of the person watching.Theatre doesn't have to be beautiful. Some of the most fantastic and thought-provoking pieces are ugly. There is an aesthetic in the staging and design- which should enhance the stories or design of the production- but it doesn't have to be beautiful. Also, the notion of beauty in the theatre is- as in life- defined by the perspective of the viewer. For me, beauty may be defined by other simplicities... stripping away all the white-noise of circumstances and just focussing on human action. That's where I find moments of beauty in theatre, where those absolutely pristine quiet pin-drop moments occur... where the audience, story and artist collide in a moment of truth. These moments of beauty dig deep into an essence. Hence, we each have our own personal aesthetic- but for me the simplicity of storytelling and the collision of human events is where beauty and aesthetic occur in theatre.Theatre always has, and always will be, important and relevant.

THE PSYCHOLOGY OF PERFORMING ARTS:THEATRE AND HUMAN EXPRESSION

Theatre is an arena in which we can mentally play, acting out our fears and fantasies in an experimental way. It excites new ideas and perspectives and provides us with rehearsal for life. In the broad sense, theatre can be taken as referring to films and TV as well as live theatre - indeed, any sort of entertainment that includes performers and audience (sometimes intertwined in complex ways) and which requires imagination to make it real.

Central to much of theatre is human conflict - the characters struggle to attain their ends against opposition, mostly from other characters. Role-playing puts us into the head of each character in turn, allowing us to see things from their viewpoint. By observing how they deal with their problems, sometimes adaptively, sometimes self-destructively, we learn lessons in how to choose among our own options. An important function of theatre is stimulation. Theatre adds magic and thrills to our mundane lives - whether it be disturbing (tragedy & horror), ridiculous (comedy) or romantic (esp. musicals). Modern civilisation has become overly safe. From time to time we need to rock the boat and test the alarms - to try out novel, challenging experiences and sample danger, albeit within a safe context. Theatre and films give us a chance to rehearse reactions to rare, dreaded occurrences such as rape, earthquake, fire or death of a loved one, helping us to cope with such events should they occur in real life. So, the audience leisure need difference between opera art performance and movie. Movie lesiure audiences visual enjoyment needs are whether the movie content is attractive or/and the or artistes their performance skills are proficient. Otherwise, the opera art performance artistes need have the actual time performance skills, because they need to perform to let their opera art performance audiences to feel visual leisure enjoyment immediate, if they can not persuade their opera art performance audiences feel happy or visual leisure feeling, otherwise, they feel boring when they are seeing their opera art performance immediately. They must decide to leave the opera art performance hall. So, all opera art performance artistes need know every opera art performance audience individual emotion, whether he/she is enjoying or boring when he/she is seeing their opera art performance on the performance hall.

What is the role of spectacle in performing arts?

Spectacle is largely a question of means, but it also brings an accent to a presentation or to the way of doing a show. At the beginning of Cirque, we were just a group of street-performers- not great acrobats, so the spectacle was little! As we went along, we were able to add artificial spectacle which was connected to the performance and enhanced with better acrobats- improving the whole experience. Now it would be very hard to go back to 1984 where we were just street-acrobats, people expect and accept spectacle from our performances now.

What is the role of the actor in theatre?

The actor is the person who tells someone else's story, he is the messenger of the story; regardless of whether that story was written by a composer, a lyricist or an author. He is the human-conduit to convey the story to the audience. His or her choices are therefore crucial in making that story as vivid as it can be. Also, the performer and his performance are the skeleton of our production. We can put muscles over this in the form of costumes and lights... we will add music, light and invoke the emotion of this skeleton by bringing it to life, but the performance is at the centre of all of this. Moreover, actors are communicators, storytellers, inventors and commentators. They have many roles in their art, depending on the story they are telling and the genre of the play. Actors are there to entertain, but also to deliver the story as the writer (or they, themselves) would want.As an actor, you are an artist. Greatness comes from the quality of the transformation, experience and how they can access and communicate emotion to effect a change in the audience.

Hence, theatre is an art-form that is meant to be heard. It is a collection of words and moments that are defined by the writer, but ultimately given voice by the actor. For me while it's always story first; the actor is the instrument for those stories coming to life. We each have our own notion of truth, but the great actors are the ones who make truth the through-line of their work. They are the ones who make the boundary between actor and character invisible-immersing themselves in the story. They are the ones who allow the audience to do the same. A great performance is not full of noise, but full of context and story. The actor must be generous, and give with abandon. Real theatre and real performance exists when you have a meeting of the performer and the audience as receiver. The audience are an active participant, theatre is a relationship between the production and the audience- audiences are not just consuming. For example, a piece of theatre is not complete until the audience is in the room. The work is changed by the presence of an audience. When you are making work you see rehearsals and so forth, but what the piece becomes when an audience joins the process translates it to another stage. Whether the audience know it or not, they are active in the process. They clarify things, deny things, join with ideas and more. Moreover, the audience are not passive consumers of theatre, it is a circular relationship.It is extremely important that an audience and a story become one. You often hear people describe the experience of 'losing themselves' in the story; I- personally- would call it 'finding yourself'. My guess would be that if you talk to the average audience member or artist, those unique moments that keep us coming back to theatre are relatively rare; yet we keep going. We want that moment where we get so immersed.. where all the people in the audience and the production come together... that is what resonates with us for years to come.

Designing a Good Theater to influence audience seeing movie or opera art performance positive emotion feeling factor

Instead of learning how to produce one good movie or opera art performance content and the artor individence performance skill and length of performance time arrangement factors, the designing a Good theater location factor will be one important factor to influence audience individual emotion. They may include as below:

Since humanity started gathering to tell stories and represent scenes from everyday life in front of an audience, the need for a space to perform such activities began to increase. Theater design developed from the open-air amphitheaters of the Greeks and Romans to the incredible array of forms we see today. Though some forms work better for particular types of performance, there is no ideal shape or size of a theater. The choice of the best form and scale depends on the functional purpose (movies, lectures, stage performances, musical presentations), the size of the staging required and the number of the audience to be accommodated. Let's see which are the basic parts that comprise a theater and the most common types of today's theater design.

1. Design a functioning Auditorium according to the type of performance and the number of the audience

It is the part of the theater accommodating the audience during the performance, sometimes known as the "house". The house can also refer to an area that is not considered playing space or backstage area. This includes the lobby, coat check, ticket counters, and restroom. The amount of space required for each auditorium depends on a number of factors but the following guides, based on modern seating design can give you an idea of the area needed

2. Keep the standard distance for a comfortable audience seating

The aisle is the space for walking with rows of seats on both sides or with rows of seats on one side and a wall on the other. In order to improve safety when the theaters are darkened during the performance, the edges of the aisles are marked with a row of small lights

3. The stage is important: choose wisely

The stage is the designated space where actors and other artists perform and the focal point for the audience. As an architectural feature, the stage may consist of a platform (often raised) or series of platforms. In some cases, these may be temporary or adjustable but in theaters and other buildings devoted to such productions, the stage is often a permanent feature. There are several types of stages that vary as to the usage and the relation of the audience to them:

Thrust theater stage :

A Stage surrounded by audience on three sides. The Fourth side serves as the background. In a typical modern arrangement: the stage is often a square or rectangular playing area, usually raised, surrounded by raked seating. Other shapes are possible; Shakespeare's Globe Theatre was a five-sided thrust stage.

For greater intimacy with the audience, go with the Thrust Stage

A thrust stage is one that extends into the audience on three sides and is connected to the backstage area by its upstage end. A thrust has the benefit of greater intimacy between the audience and performers than a proscenium while retaining the utility of a backstage area. The audience in a thrust stage theater may view the stage from three or more sides.

End Stage:

A Thrust stage extended wall to wall, like a thrust stage with audience on just one side, i.e. the front."Backstage" is behind the background wall. There is no real wingspace to the sides, although there may be entrances located there. An example of a modern end stage is a music hall, where the background walls surround the playing space on three sides. Like a thrust stage, scenery serves primarily as background, rather than surrounding the acting space.

Arena Theatre stage:

A central stage surrounded by audience on all sides. The stage area is often raised to improve sightlines.

The Proscenium Stage or End Stage :

It is the most common type of stage and it is also called a picture frame stage. Its primary feature is a large opening, the proscenium arch through which the audience views the performance. The audience directly faces the stage and views only one side of the scene. Often, a stage may extend in front of the proscenium arch which offers additional playing area to the actors. This area is referred to as the apron. Underneath and in front of the apron is sometimes an orchestra pit which is used by musicians during musicals and operas.

Flexible theater stage:

Sometimes called a "Black Box" theater, these stages are often big empty boxes painted black inside. Stage and seating not fixed. Instead, each can be altered to suit the needs of the play or the whim of the director.

Keep your theater flexible

Flexible stage theaters are those that do not establish a fixed relationship between the stage and the house. They can be put into any of the standard theater forms or any of the variations of those. Usually, there is no physical distinction between the stage and the auditorium and the audience is either standing, intermingling with the performance or sitting on the main floor.

Profile Theatres stage:

Often used in "found space" theaters, i.e. theaters made by converted from other spaces. The Audience is often placed on risers to either side of the playing space, with little or no audience on either end of the "stage". Actors are staged in profile to the audience. It is often the most workable option for long, narrow spaces like "store fronts". Scenically, a profile theater is most like an arena stage; some staging as background is possible at ends, which are essentially sides. A non-theatrical form of the profile stage is a basketball arena, if no-one is seated behind the hoops.

Sports Arenas stage :

Sports arenas often serve as venues for Music Concerts. In form they resemble very large arena stage (more accurately the arena stage resembles a sports arena), but with a retangular floorplan. When used for concert, a temporary stage area often is set up as an end-stage at one end of the floor, and the rest of the floor and the stands become the audience. Arenas have their own terminology

Keep the scenery low for better visibility

In the Theater in the round or the Arena Stage Theater, the stage is located in the center of the audience, with the audience members facing it from all sides. The audience is placed close to the action, which provides a feeling of intimacy and involvement. However, this type puts major restrictions on the amount and kind of visual spectacle that can be provided for a performance, because scenery more than a few feet tall will block the audience view of the action taking place onstage.

4. Sound quality is as important as visibility

Although theater performances are a visual medium, poor sound quality will ruin even the better plays. The sound is an area often overlooked but, just as you need good sightlines, you also need good sound-lines. Apart from the obvious comfort and size considerations, External sound insulation (how many times have you heard traffic noise, trains or building works over the soundtrack of the film you are watching?) Internal sound insulation – this is particularly important with multiple screens where a loud soundtrack can leak into the adjoining auditorium.Services and equipment noise control – noises such as air conditioning, lifts, toilets and projection equipment need to be controlled. Acoustics – acoustic design in theaters should be considered from feasibility stage – location, auditorium planning etc. through to final commissioning.

What is theatre's economic role?

Every single independent tourist review that is written about reasons why people should come to the UK and London starts with heritage/royalty and then immediately moves on to theatre.... Specifically theatre.... not the arts, not entertainment, not shopping, not restaurants... the theatre. Alongside the fact that theatre employs many people in many diverse and different jobs, it's also a great regenerator of town-centres. If you speak to any government or local-government official that is trying to regenerate cities and towns further, theatres are at the centre. From time to time I get interviewed by an unnamed newspaper about the death of the West End. I always offer to take the journalist around London in a taxi where I can show them boarded up shops, boarded up offices, boarded up factories and boarded up pubs.

However, theatre is growing globally, and people want it globally. How the work of theatre develop will be a fascinating blend of cultures, it's an incredible opportunity. We currently have three proposals from Shanghai asking us to build, operate and convert theatres as a central core-magnet to retail, residential and other developments. This is alongside conversations we are having in Korea, Hong Kong and more. Around the world, more theatres are being built now than at any other time in history. Theatre will lose the London and New York concentration. Hamburg, Vienna, Melbourne and Sydney are already great theatre cities. Hong Kong is growing into a great theatre destination too. There is also a huge opportunity across Canada and other territories. I see theatre essentially following an upward trajectory in terms of number of cities and venues.

People worldwide now acknowledge theatre is good for society economically and socially.

What does the next 50 years hold for theatre or opera art performance leisure need ? I think the essential core of theatre.... the unique selling proposition of being there to see it, having to perform in a space... will remain the same.... However what that core is saying and doing will depend on the message and story of the artists of the future. The activity of theatre has lasted for many thousands of years. As long as human beings have the need to hear stories, and to tell stories, it will remain. We're in very difficult times at the moment in terms of funding. This does however mean that we tend to get better at what we do. The work gets tougher, leaner and better. I would hope however that regional-theatre funding improves in the future, and we're left with a secure theatre network.

In fact, Theatre is ultimately about conflict between people and circumstances... you can wrap it in a different package and bow, but these principles have remained the same for hundreds of years.In the off-Broadway scene of the 1960s, you saw a trend of self-generating theatre in store-fronts and unusual venues. They were still going after the essence of theatre, but taking it everywhere. If you look today at the influence of technology in theatre, we are now able to do some of the things we used to do by hand- but more easily... for example, throwing a light cue by computer rather than moving dimmers by hand. However, technology gives us more tools to get to the core event, but ultimately the fierce passion the artist has to reveal the story is what powers the theatre.

How do artists cope with the mental pressures of perfection?

I would contest that we all have one or two 'issues' with our mental health, perhaps that is just the normal being of being a human. The discipline of ballet gives you the ability to manage your emotions, and an outlet for them. Ballet is a way to go through your emotions with the permission to exploit your frustrations, investigating them, using them and exposing them.Society faces dangers when people have doubts and questions, and cannot investigate them. When people hold-on to their emotions, and don't become malleable to them.. they become fragile, and can break, like glass.

What is the role of digital technology , how it can influence audience emotion from online movie or opera art performance online watching channel in the modern world?

Digital technology is making us insular. We think we have relationships through Facebook, Twitter and Instagram, but they are not real. There is no physical connection. We are human, we need physical connection. Participating in public performance, where you are a part of something with other people is more important than ever. It's more important than ever that we encourage young people into the arts in a meaningful way where they feel they want to go, and can afford to go. Right now, we can't even get young people through the door- and that's hard.

Looking even further to the future, we are entering the world of artificial intelligence and robotics. There is a chance that machines will be performing many of our world's most physical tasks. Wouldn't it be better if we guarantee the future of our children with creativity? That's the one thing machines can't compete with us on. Human beings will live maybe 100 years, and we leave school when we're 16, 17, 18. We need to teach kids to enjoy learning, to be curious, and to always want to learn. Not one iota of what they will become can be taught by us. The most important thing is that children enjoy the process of discovery. The more we encourage creativity, the more digital technology encourage young age audience group to imagine alternate realities when they can see movie or opera art performance from internet channel, the more our futures will all be brighter.

How has art changed your world-view?

Art has changed my world-view completely. I have travelled the world, not for tourism but to work. I have worked with so many different people, from so many different cultures and backgrounds and I have had my mind opened about humanity.I don't feel that I am a particular person from a particular part of the world. I was born somewhere, grew-up somewhere else, and lived in a few more places. I am a person of the world. Art has allowed me to live with myself, and to make sense of the fragility of humanity's desires and traits. I'm just a human being, and art has given me the space to be OK with that.

What inspires you as an artist? How you are as artist , you feel you may perform your movie or opera art performance to attract audience attention? Working with choreographers and producing stuff that really makes people think, and changes their ideas, and takes them to another place... that's powerful for me. for dance performance example, dance in itself is a social skill that everybody should appreciate and enjoy, our bodies are made to move. If you choose to specialise in the field- you're like an athlete. You have to be built for the technique. The role of the body is important and for dancers, it's about the joints, flexibility and muscular strength. The proportions of the body are also important; that's part of the aesthetic, and you can't help that- this is a visual art. How would be your art performance message to the next generation? You really have to devote your life to theatre. It doesn't mean you can't have a family and so forth... but it isn't like some activities in life where you can get a healthy work-life balance, as much as we would like to encourage it. Theatre is your life as well as your work, and if that doesn't fit with you, then theatre isn't right for you. Whatever your talent... music, movement, whatever... if you have the drive to continue and develop and become a great performer then you should. It's a lot of work- my father used to tell me that in life you need a little bit of talent, but lots of hard work. If you have a little talent, prepare yourself for hard work to develop it, and you may attain greatness; but don't forget that the road to greatness is long. You should make the work that tells the stories you feel are important to you and your generation. The role of a theatre maker is to tell the stories of our lives. You should try and grab the whole of the gamut of emotions, it's not just to entertain. The mix and bravery by which you grab those emotions makes theatre exciting. Moreover, you must be fearless and brave. You must be willing to express what you feel, and to do that with thought. People have a fear of expression, and we must encourage them to do the hard, hard work it takes to overcome this and know they are empowered to make work. All great work comes from this principle, new forms are made, new theatre is created.... When someone stops to write... or stops to raise some money? those are the moments where greatness is created. Also, you have to be curious and learn as much as you can from as many people as you can. You can even learn from people who don't know what they're doing; at least you will then know how not to do something. You have to be kind to yourself. You do not have to suffer or punish yourself to be a great artist. The sooner you can accept yourself, the sooner you can progress and discover what you're capable of. Life is so short, and goes so fast, you have to enjoy it. Life will throw you in so many directions, and goals are not the end; they are simply gateways to more questions, and this process of discovering answers and new questions is never complete, that's life. People have a lot of inhibitions, and are hugely preoccupied with what other people are thinking. Dance gives you a space to forget that, and enjoy being you. I always think you should dance with others, but it's amazing how happy you can be dancing on your own. For me however, the entertainment and enjoyment is dancing with friends or even strangers. Dancing breaks-down so many barriers, and makes you more comfortable with people around you. People let their guard-down when they dance, and it opens a lot of doors for communications. I have a fitness and dance programme that we take into state-schools. We let kids try anything they want in dance and let their creativity flow. They can do any genre from around the world- the aim is to find something that they can connect with to give them a feel of what dance can do. When you see the reaction? My God, it's the happiest they've ever been! They're testing their bodies like they've never done before, and finding skills that they didn't think they had. It gives them a space to enjoy being themselves, without peer-pressure, without the stresses that can impact their lives so negatively at this early stage.

However, art is one of the most valuable assets of human society, yet the truth is that while we may attach art to a time and a place; it's true provenance and relevance remain intangible. We can look at the raw materials (the paint, the instrument?, the composition (the brush strokes, the music) or even the act of consumption (viewing, listing? – but the thing that we observe only becomes art within us. The phenomenon of art emerges within the intangible mix of experience and cultural inputs that create our mind. A fact not lost on the ancient Greeks who simultaneously originated the concepts of philosophy (the love of wisdom)

and theatre (the place for viewing) c.6th century B.C.
The images of other arts are constituted in quite different ways. This engagement has a metaphysical aspect in that the image between the performer and the audience adds up to more than the sum of its various parts. A materialist criticism that does not recognise these 'metaphysical' qualities of theatre is lacking critical force. For the 'beyond physical', the numinous, the spirit, the aura of art, however it is described is a material response to art not just ideological or 'imagined'. This 'something more' than the thing itself is attested to by too many people without deference to gender, race or class. And to ignore it, as though it will go away, and leave us with the quantified, the material and the manipulable, in the name of dogmatic sectarian objectives, is to impoverish the terms on which theatre might be most valuably and pleasurably thought and practiced. This metaphysics of theatre is what is not seen, beyond the practiced, beyond the mind's eye it remains unwritten. It is the domain which both makes theatre worthwhile and simultaneously jeopardises its effects. For it is in this hinterland of the undocumented and discreet that the fallacies of theatre are nourished. This 'something more' of the image does not disconnect the experience of theatre from its place of performance, nor from the everyday. Theatre remains bound by its context precisely through the unique relationship images create between audience, performer and everyday life." He adds that, "To value theatre, is to value life, not to escape from it. The everyday is at once the most habitual and demanding dimension of life which theatre has most responsibility to. Theatre does not tease people out of their everyday lives like other expressions of wish fulfilment but reminds them who they are and what is worth living and changing in their lives

every day." (Theatre and Every Day Life, 1993)
The concept of everyday life here is critical. Human beings are cursed with the knowledge of agency. We know without a shadow of a doubt that our immediate experiences are limited simply to ourselves. In many philosophies this is even manifest as the discussion of how one is trapped in the body- able to only experience the substantive world which we have ingested through our limited senses. With this in mind, we quickly see the real power of theatre. Prof. Erin Hurley describes how, "Theatre allows for and offers vicarious experience: the experience of someone else experiencing something?We know that witnessing another's actions and emotional experiences can create the same neurological imprint as doing or feeling them oneself. Joseph Roach provocatively recasts the history of theatre in terms of the good of what he calls 'synthetic experience', a cognate to vicarious experience. The theatre is a port of entry into another's life and another kind of living." (Theatre and Feeling, 2010)
On conclusion, art is the medium by which we- as human beings- are able to relate to each other. Art allows us to understand things that are more than ourselves, and imagine life through the agency of others. Theatre- as perhaps the most human of all the arts- has the profound ability to engage us immediately in the experience of someone else's agency- at any point in time, at any place. It breaks down the loneliness of being a self, and allows one to realise that not only are there others- but that the self can be them too. Art Business Charity conflict creativity culture. So, any movie or opera art performance businessmen need to educate our next generation needs to considerate art performance movie or opera art performance lesisure industry needs to be continued to develop in order to let

they can learn more new art culture and build positive charter role in our society, then crimes number will be influenced to reduce when they can see any health movie or opera art performance after they buy tickets to enter cinemas or opera art performance hall and let they feel that it is valuable economic spending time to see the movie or the opera art leisure performance.

9 798887 332567

Printed by Libri Plureos GmbH in Hamburg, Germany